## Nature's Freak Show: Ugly Beasts

# THE REPULSIVE NAKED MOLE RAT

BY JANEY LEVY

Gareth Stevens
PUBLISHING

Please visit our website, www.garethstevens.com. For a free color catalog of all our high-quality books, call toll free 1-800-542-2595 or fax 1-877-542-2596.

Cataloging-in-Publication Data

Names: Levy, Janey.
Title: The repulsive naked mole rat / Janey Levy.
Description: New York : Gareth Stevens Publishing, 2020. | Series: Nature's freak show: ugly beasts | Includes glossary and index.
Identifiers: ISBN 9781538246184 (pbk.) | ISBN 9781538246207 (library bound) | ISBN 9781538246191 (6 pack)
Subjects: LCSH: Naked mole rat--Juvenile literature.
Classification: LCC QL737.R628 L48 2020 | DDC 599.35--dc23

First Edition

Published in 2020 by
**Gareth Stevens Publishing**
111 East 14th Street, Suite 349
New York, NY 10003

Copyright © 2020 Gareth Stevens Publishing

Designer: Katelyn E. Reynolds
Editor: Monika Davies

Photo credits: Cover, pp. 1, 5, 9, 11, 13, 21 Neil Bromhall/Shutterstock.com; cover, pp. 1-24 (curtain background) Africa Studio/Shutterstock.com; cover, pp. 1-24 (wood sign) Rawpixel.com/Shutterstock.com; cover, pp. 1-24 (marquee signs) iunewind/Shutterstock.com; p. 7 R. Andrew Odum/Photolibrary/Getty Images; p. 15 belizar/Shutterstock.com; p. 17 Steve Gorton/Dorling Kindersley/Getty Images; p. 19 Karen Tweedy-Holmes/Corbis Documentary/Getty Images.

All rights reserved. No part of this book may be reproduced in any form without permission in writing from the publisher, except by a reviewer.

Printed in the United States of America

Some of the images in this book illustrate individuals who are models. The depictions do not imply actual situations or events.

CPSIA compliance information: Batch #CW20GS: For further information contact Gareth Stevens, New York, New York at 1-800-542-2595.

# CONTENTS

Meet the Naked Mole Rat .................................................. 4
Bizarre Body ................................................................. 6
A Curious Type of Colony ................................................ 8
Providing for Pups ........................................................ 10
Mealtime ..................................................................... 12
No Oxygen? No Problem! ............................................... 14
Defying Disease ........................................................... 16
Above the Aging Process ............................................... 18
The Outstanding Naked Mole Rat .................................... 20
Glossary ...................................................................... 22
For More Information .................................................... 23
Index .......................................................................... 24

Words in the glossary appear in bold type the first time they are used in the text.

# MEET THE NAKED MOLE RAT

You're likely wondering: What exactly is a naked mole rat? Is it a mole? Or, is it a rat? Well, it isn't either one! It's a **rodent**, like a rat. However, the naked mole rat is not closely related to rats. It's actually more closely related to porcupines and guinea pigs, or small animals kept as pets.

The naked mole rat is a strange-looking animal. But the naked mole rat has captured scientists' attention because of its many unusual features. You'll discover more inside this book.

**STRANGE BUT TRUE!**
Naked mole rats may look hairless. But they do have fine hairs on their head and tail, as well as hairs between their toes.

NAKED MOLE RATS ARE ALSO NAMED SAND PUPPIES OR DESERT MOLE RATS.

# BIZARRE BODY

Naked mole rats don't look like any rodent you've ever seen. For starters, they're mostly bare. Pinkish, wrinkled skin covers their tube-shaped body. They have thin, tiny legs and a short, skinny tail.

The naked mole rat's head is short and wide. Two upper and two lower teeth stick out of their mouth. Their ears are just holes. They have very small eyes and are mostly blind. But naked mole rats have a good sense of smell. And, their few hairs help them feel what's around them.

**STRANGE BUT TRUE!** Naked mole rats have long teeth that move separately of each other. They can move their teeth like chopsticks, pushing them apart and pulling them back together. That's wild!

THE TEETH OF A NAKED MOLE RAT KEEP GROWING THROUGHOUT THEIR ENTIRE LIFE. BUT SINCE THEY CHEW ON HARD OBJECTS, THEIR TEETH STAY WORN DOWN AND NEVER GET TOO LONG.

# A CURIOUS TYPE OF COLONY

Many kinds of animals live in groups. But naked mole rats live in a special kind of group called a eusocial (yoo-SOH-shuhl) colony. Ants and bees live in eusocial colonies, but it's really unusual for **mammals** to live in such colonies. Only one other mammal does, and it's also a type of mole rat.

So, what's a eusocial colony? It's a group where only one female—called the queen—produces babies. The other colony members work to take care of the colony.

**STRANGE BUT TRUE!** Naked mole rats live in burrows and tunnels in dry areas of eastern Africa. The tunnels have special rooms for nesting and eating. There's even a toilet room!

NAKED MOLE RAT TUNNELS CAN BE 2.5 MILES (4 KM) LONG! THEY DIG THEIR TUNNELS USING THEIR LONG TEETH. THE HAIRS BETWEEN THEIR TOES HELP THEM BRUSH THE DIRT BEHIND THEM.

# PROVIDING FOR PUPS

The naked mole rat queen has babies about 70 days after **mating** with a few special males in the colony. She can have up to 27 babies, or pups, at a time! But she usually gives birth to about 12 pups.

The pups stay in the nesting room. The queen nurses them, and worker naked mole rats care for them. The pups grow up fast. They start eating solid food when they're about 2 weeks old. They're wandering the tunnels within weeks and working in just a few months.

### STRANGE BUT TRUE!
A colony also has workers and soldiers. The workers are in charge of finding food, digging tunnels, and caring for the pups. Soldiers fight off predators that enter the tunnels.

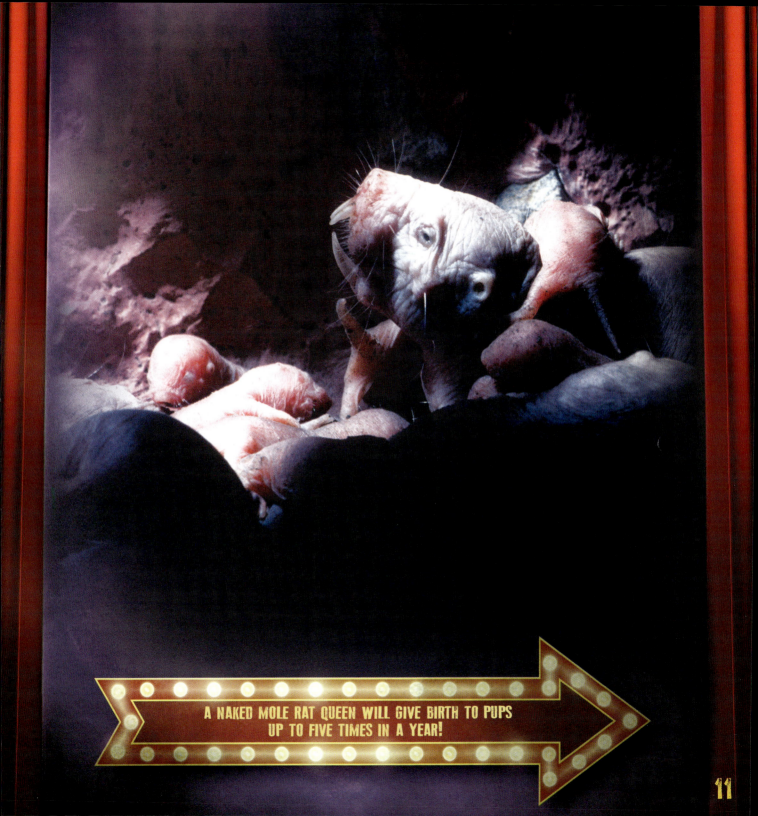

A NAKED MOLE RAT QUEEN WILL GIVE BIRTH TO PUPS UP TO FIVE TIMES IN A YEAR!

# MEALTIME

Since naked mole rats live in tunnels under the ground, what do they find to eat? Well, they eat large plant roots that grow into their tunnels. They use their strong front teeth to eat these roots.

These roots have a lot of matter called cellulose, which is hard to **digest**. The naked mole rats have bacteria in their gut to help them digest the cellulose. But to make sure they don't lose **nutrients** in their waste, they also eat their own poop. Yuck!

**STRANGE BUT TRUE!** Naked mole rats don't eat the entire root of a plant. They leave part of it behind so the plant stays alive and can supply meals down the road.

NAKED MOLE RATS DON'T DRINK WATER. THEY GET ALL THE WATER THEY NEED FROM THEIR FOOD.

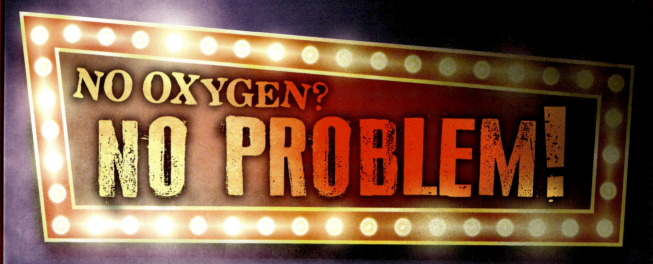

# NO OXYGEN? NO PROBLEM!

Naked mole rats need to breathe **oxygen** to survive, just like other mammals. But scientists have discovered that naked mole rats can survive at oxygen levels so low that other mammals would die.

To stay alive, mammals must turn matter from their food called glucose into **energy** for their body. They need oxygen to do that. But when there's no oxygen, naked mole rats use a different matter called fructose from their food instead. Turning fructose into energy doesn't require oxygen. That's a striking skill!

**STRANGE BUT TRUE!** Scientists put naked mole rats into a space with no oxygen. The naked mole rats survived 18 minutes without oxygen!

Earth's air is about 21 percent oxygen. Naked mole rats survive easily breathing air that's made of only 5 percent oxygen.

# DEFYING DISEASE

Naked mole rats can avoid getting cancer, which is a deadly **disease**. Cancer happens when one of the body's cells multiplies out of control. This crowds out the body's healthy cells and stops the body from working well.

Cancer cells often collect together to form masses called tumors. But naked mole rats have a sugar called hyaluronan in their body that keeps cells from bunching up together. They also have a **gene** that causes cancer cells to destroy themselves.

**STRANGE BUT TRUE!** The special sugar in a naked mole rat's body helps the cancer-killing gene do its job. When the special sugar turns the gene "on," the gene then destroys the cancer cells!

THE SPECIAL SUGAR IN NAKED MOLE RATS EXISTS IN ALL ANIMALS. BUT NAKED MOLE RATS HAVE A LOT MORE OF THIS SPECIAL SUGAR COMPARED TO OTHER ANIMALS.

# Above the Aging Process

For humans and all other mammals, the chance of dying increases with age. A math **equation** called the Gompertz law explains this idea. The equation states as you get older, your risk of dying gets higher and higher. But naked mole rats break this law!

Unusually for small rodents, naked mole rats can live for more than 30 years. And, even the oldest naked mole rats show few signs of aging. They're not more likely to die than young naked mole rats.

**STRANGE BUT TRUE!** Once a naked mole rat turns 6 months old, its daily chance of dying is only about one in 10,000. It stays that way for the rest of the animal's life.

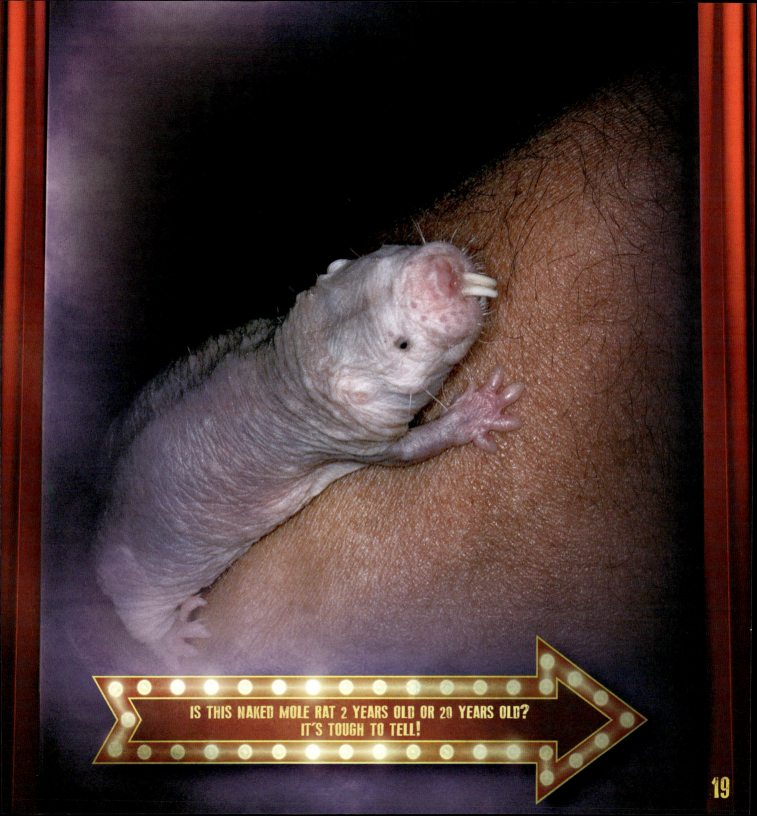

IS THIS NAKED MOLE RAT 2 YEARS OLD OR 20 YEARS OLD? IT'S TOUGH TO TELL!

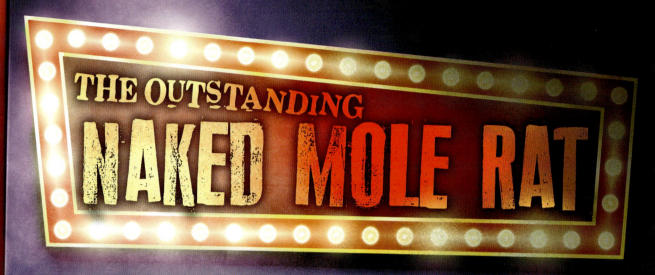

# THE OUTSTANDING NAKED MOLE RAT

By now it should be clear naked mole rats are pretty amazing animals. They may look really weird, but their unusual features make them truly special. And, there are even more surprising facts to discover about these creatures.

The members of a naked mole rat colony need to be able to recognize each other. They all roll around in their toilet room so they all smell the same. Ew! Check out the next page to learn more fun facts about naked mole rats.

# FUN FACTS

- Their lips close behind their teeth. This keeps dirt out of their mouth!
- When a female becomes queen, she grows longer.
- Females often fight to death to become queen.
- They can run at the same pace forwards and backwards.
- They don't feel some kinds of pain.
- They can't keep a regular body temperature. They stick together in close packs to stay warm.
- They communicate with each other using at least 17 different sounds.

# GLOSSARY

**burrow:** a hole made by an animal in which it lives or hides

**communicate:** to share ideas and feelings through sounds and motions

**digest:** to break down food inside the body so that the body can use it

**disease:** illness

**energy:** power used to do work

**equation:** a statement showing two mathematical statements are equal

**gene:** a tiny part of a cell that is passed along from one living thing to its offspring

**mammal:** a warm-blooded animal that has a backbone and hair, breathes air, and feeds milk to its young

**mate:** to come together to make babies

**nutrient:** something a living thing needs to grow and stay alive

**oxygen:** a colorless, odorless gas that many animals, including people, need to breathe

**rodent:** a small, furry animal with large front teeth, such as a mouse or rat

**temperature:** how hot or cold something is

# FOR MORE INFORMATION

## BOOKS

Hansen, Grace. *Weird Animals to Shock You!* Minneapolis, MN: Abdo Kids, 2017.

Hudd, Emily. *Naked Mole-Rats.* North Mankato, MN: Capstone Press, 2020.

Munro, Roxie. *Rodent Rascals.* New York, NY: Holiday House, 2018

## WEBSITES

**Naked Mole-Rats**
www.akronzoo.org/naked-mole-rats
Read up on naked mole rats and see some photos on this website.

**Naked Mole-Rat**
www.philadelphiazoo.org/Animals/Mammals/Other-Mammals/Naked-Mole-Rat.aspx
Find out how naked mole rats live at the zoo and in the wild here.

**Naked Mole-Rat Cam**
nationalzoo.si.edu/webcams/naked-mole-rat-cam
Watch the naked mole rats on camera at the Smithsonian Institution's National Zoo on this site.

**Publisher's note to educators and parents:** Our editors have carefully reviewed these websites to ensure that they are suitable for students. Many websites change frequently, however, and we cannot guarantee that a site's future contents will continue to meet our high standards of quality and educational value. Be advised that students should be closely supervised whenever they access the Internet.

Africa 8
aging 18
bacteria 12
body 6, 14, 16
cancer 16
cellulose 12
colony 8, 10, 20
ears 6
eating 8, 10
eyes 6
food 10, 13, 14
fructose 14
glucose 14
Gompertz law 18
guinea pigs 4
gut 12
hairs 4, 6, 9

head 4, 6
hyaluronan 16
nesting room 10
predators 10
pups 10, 11
queen 8, 10, 11
roots 12
scientists 4, 14
skin 6
smell 6, 20
soldiers 10
tail 4, 6
teeth 6, 7, 9, 12
toilet room 8, 20
tunnels 8, 9, 10, 12
water 13
workers 10